AF351163

Draw Chester's Challenges

by Rachell Freed

Draw Chester's Challenges

By Rachell Freed

Liz Mitchell, Editor

Houston L Bell, Jr., Cover painting

Copyright © 2024 by Rachell Freed

www.ChestersChallenges.com

authorrachellfreed@gmail.com

Twitter @authorrachellfreed

Instagram @authorrachellfreed

Facebook Rachell Freed

979-8-8692-2832-1

All rights reserved. This book is protected by the copyright laws of the United States of America. This book may not be copied or reprinted for commercial gain or profit. However, short quotations or occasional page copying for personal or group study is encouraged. Printed in the United States of America.

In a little village nestled between rolling hills lived a small, fuzzy creature named
Chester. Something was different about him. He had no hair!

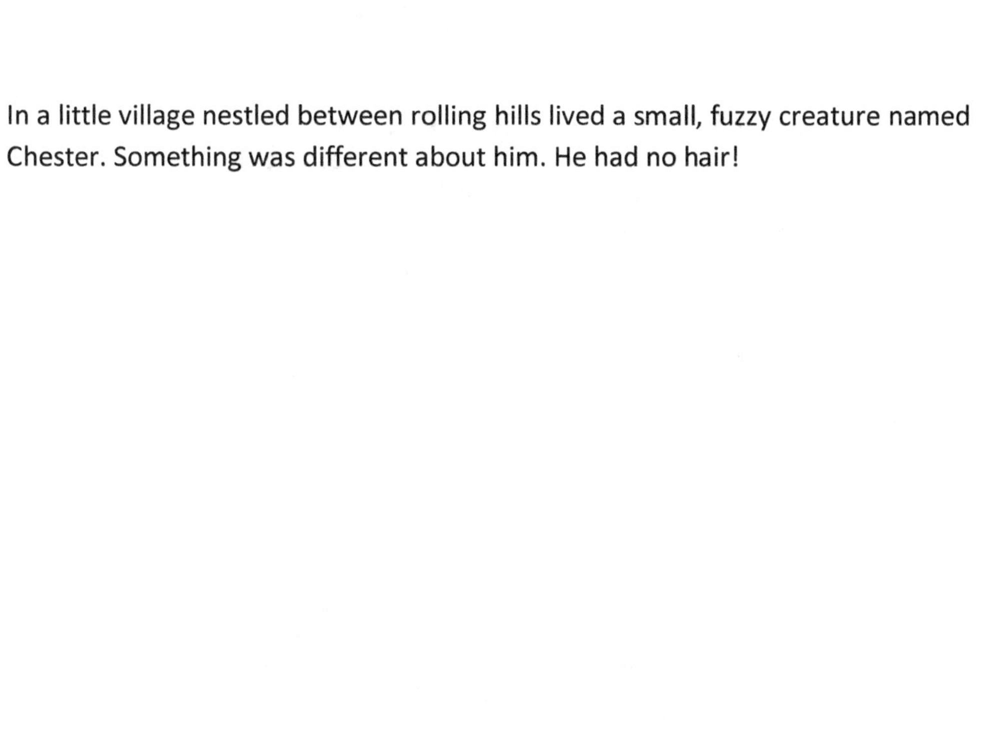

Draw Chester with each of his challenges.

Chester's cozy den was filled with bright smiles and laughter. His few teeth sparkled like tiny pearls as he joined in the playful chatter of his friends.

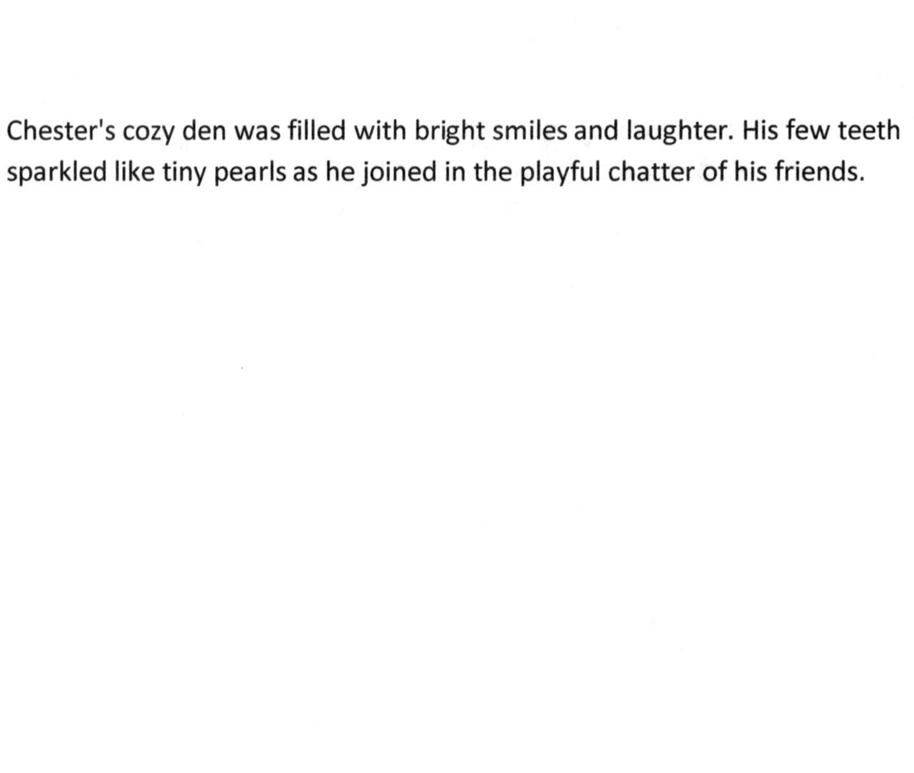

Draw Chester showing his teeth.

However, Chester faced another challenge. His hearing wasn't as sharp as everyone else's. He would tilt his head curiously, using his other senses to explore the world around him.

Draw Chester exploring the world.

One sunny morning, while Chester munched on his soft breakfast, he
realized that he couldn't nibble on hard foods like his pals because he did not
have a lower jaw.

Draw Chester eating.

Despite his small stature, Chester had a big heart. He would lend a helping paw to anyone in need, and his courage inspired his friends to be kind also.

Draw Chester with a friend.

As time went by, Chester began to grow new hair and decided to embrace his distinct appearance.

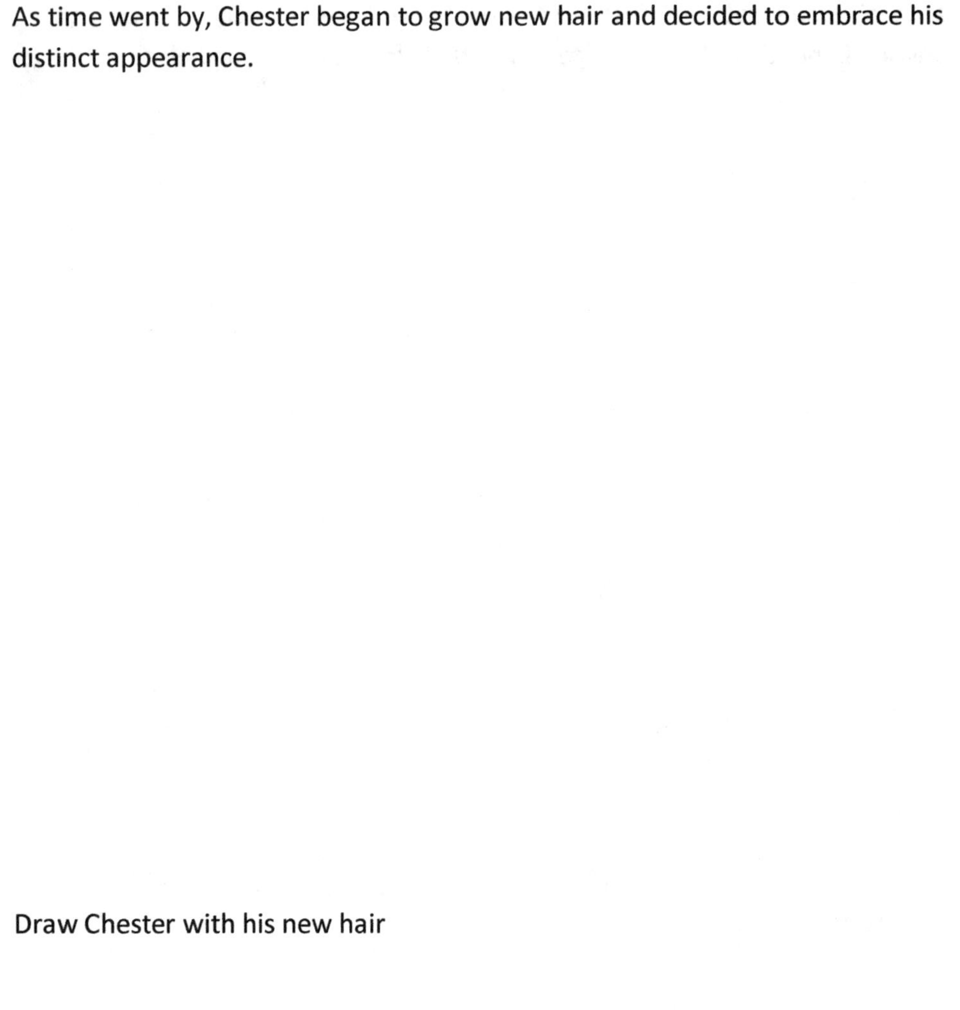

Draw Chester with his new hair

Chester experimented with new colorful clothes that showcased his one-of-a-kind style.

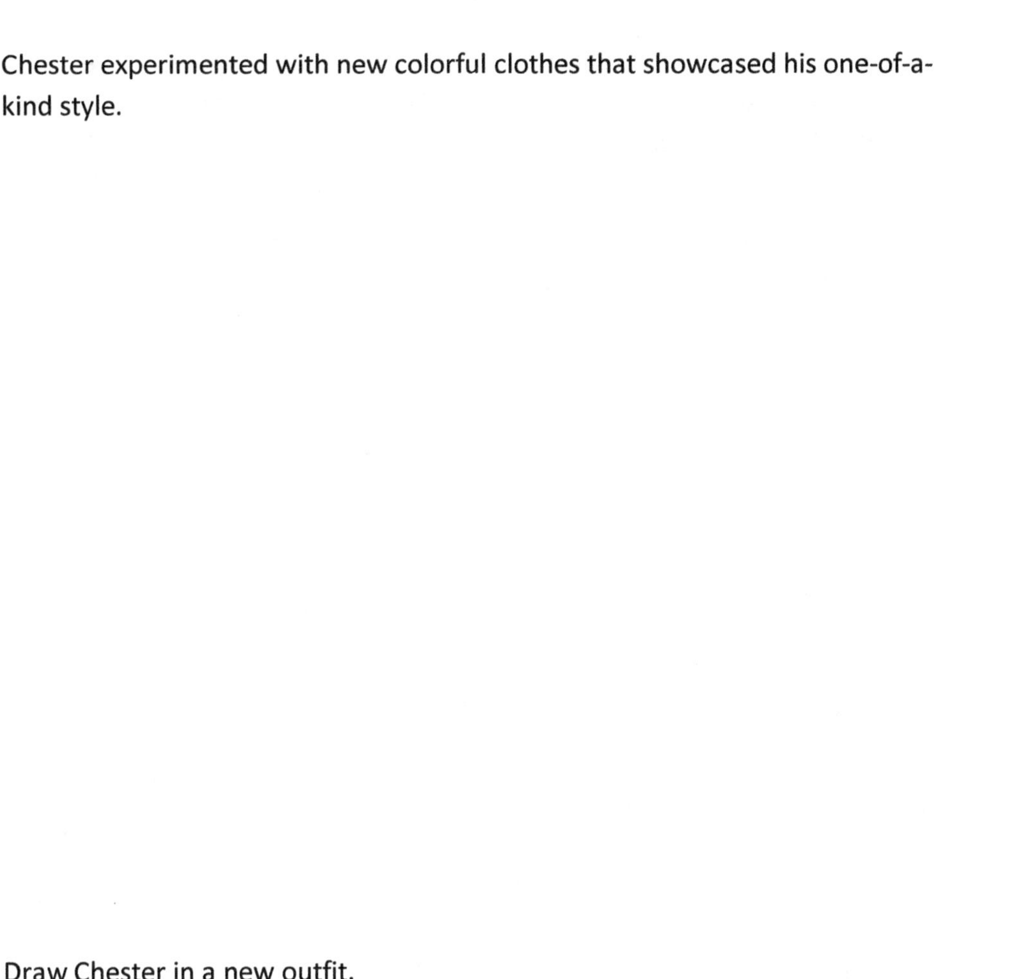

Draw Chester in a new outfit.

Whenever Chester felt pure happiness, his tail would wag like a flag in the wind. His tail-wagging dance spread joy to all, teaching his friends that being different was a gift to be celebrated.

Draw a happy Chester.

With a heart full of laughter and lessons of friendship, Chester's story continued. His journey taught everyone that embracing uniqueness is a wonderful adventure and that true friends accept each other for who they are.

Draw Chester's Challenges is a story of a tiny rescue dog who teaches that it is ok to be different. He is the emotional support dog of author Rachell Freed. She first published her own story in *He Is Forever With Me*. Learn about her at www.HeIsForeverWithMe.com

www.ChestersChallenges.com

979-8-8692-2832-1

www.ingramcontent.com/pod-product-compliance
Lightning Source LLC
Chambersburg PA
CBHW081923120726
47996CB00010B/3446